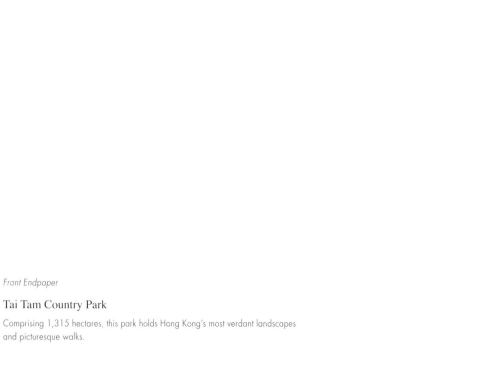

Tai Tam Country Park

Comprising 1,315 hectares, this park holds Hong Kong's most verdant landscapes and picturesque walks.

Hong Kong

The Diversity of Cultures 2

A Photographic Portfolio by Fumio Okada

City of Tiny Lights

Aerial shot taken at night from the International Commerce Centre's (ICC) viewing platform, the Sky100. In this magnificent photo, showing almost a 180-degree view of Hong Kong Island, the expanse of quiet, deep indigo water reflects colours cast by a multitude of lights.

Twinkling Harbour

Spanning Wanchai to Central, buildings lining the Hong Kong harbour sparkle like jewels against the night sky.

Hong Kong THE DIVERSITY OF CULTURES 2

Lion Rock

Taken right at the foot of Lion Rock. In this up-close view, the magnificent 495-metre Lion Rock
resembles a lion sitting with its head facing west, as if watching guard over Hong Kong.

Temple Rooftop

Shimmering in the sunlight, this traditional Chinese-style rooftop is part of the Western Monastery in Lo Wai Village. The temple is surrounded by trees, flowers and ponds.

Rock and Sea

Steep cliff coastlines serve as a backdrop to sculptured rocks rising from the sea. The Hong Kong
National Geopark boasts stunning land and sea forms.

Old and New

Juxtaposed against Hong Kong's modern skyline, a traditional Chinese junk carrying sightseers slowly sails alongside a small wooden fishing boat, whose occupants dangle handheld lines to catch fish.

Dragon Dance

One of the longest dragons in Hong Kong captured at full thrust in Shamshuipo.
Run by an intense team the speed of the dance was super fast. Seen at festive celebrations of all
kinds, the Dragon Dance is a colourful and exciting spectacle.

Explosion of Colours

Under this spectacular fireworks display Victoria Harbour is illuminated in myriad colours. Each year hordes of spectators come to witness Hong Kong's Chinese New Year celebrations.

Hong Kong THE DIVERSITY OF CULTURES 2

Book Cover

The magnificent nighttime view of Hong Kong from the Peak.

Hong Kong

The Diversity of Cultures 2

A Photographic Portfolio by Fumio Okada

Preface

To the millions who visit each year, Hong Kong is a frantic city of shiny skyscrapers, spectacular harbour views, shopping malls, bright lights and pulsating streets. It's a realistic snapshot but, is only one frame of the bigger picture.

Behind its glitzy facade, Hong Kong has a gentler side composed of lush green landscapes, serene ancient temples and quaint villages. The glamorous and the naturally beautiful, the old and the new, coexist in ways that give Hong Kong an identity all its own.

A certainty of modern Hong Kong is that the city skyline is constantly changing. New high-rise buildings replace the old, faster, wider roads are carved out of reclaimed land, and ever-higher skyscrapers jostle for prime position along the harbour front.

In this second edition of The Diversity of Cultures, photographer Fumio Okada has sought out new angles in which to demonstrate this evolution. From the stunning panoramic photos of Victoria Harbour taken in the 1970s and 2012 to the dizzying aerial views now afforded by the International Commerce Centre (ICC).

Stunning cityscapes are juxtaposed with an exploration into Hong Kong's countryside, where the lush tropical landscape of Tai Tam Park contrasts the granite face of Lion Rock. The seas and waterways that serve as a lifeline through the city are photographed from inspiring angles; the engineering miracle bridges that cross them akin to modern-day sculptures.

Hong Kong's rich cultural heritage is also captured in new found ways. In the New Territories, intimate portraits of village elders descending from the Hakka people are beautifully immortalised alongside new generations. The glowing light in which the Li Cheung Uk Han Tomb is captured draws the viewer in as if to point out that Hong Kong has a history that pre-dates British colonialism, which is also documented here.

Vibrant, time-old traditions such as the Dragon Boat races, the Bun Festival, Lion and Dragon Dances are taken with a certainty that only years of experience in shooting fast action with patience can achieve. Endurance is also required when photographing places of worship, regardless of whether they are dedicated to deities such as Tin Hau, the goddess revered for protecting those at sea, Buddhist and Taoist temples, or churches.

Hong Kong is a multicultural society, bursting with colours, heritage and pride. In this book, Fumio Okada has endeavoured to capture its myriad idiosyncrasies with integrity, and liberate each image through the use of both film and digital photography.

Martine Beale

Photographer's Note

When Hong Kong was handed over to China in 1997, many border areas between the two were restricted to the general public. In February 2012 a small part of a restricted area in Sha Tau Kok close to the border of China was opened. This recently opened village is just a very small part of the New Territories and hopefully there will be further openings in the near future.

There are many Han descendants, or Hakka clans, living in the New Territories. It is interesting to note that these Hakkas, who have lived in Sha Tau Kok for hundreds of years, are more tender and gentle than the Hakkas who reside in other parts of the territory.

The completion of the new landmark ICC has gained much attention. The popular observation platform on the 100th floor of this 108-storey skyscraper provides a stunning 360-degree panoramic view of Hong Kong. Clouds often sit low on the harbour blotting out its spectacular views, making it advisable to check visibility status before visiting.

Many of Hong Kong's smaller islands are surrounded by crags, natural rock formations that have evolved over thousands of years, and are being preserved for future generations. Many of these can only be viewed by boat from a distance where it is hard to see details clearly. Capturing images of these rocks proved to be a challenge when using a single hand-held camera on a boat rocking on the waves.

As the 35mm digital camera seemed a popular and handy choice, I recently started to use one. I found it quite limiting, although there are ongoing improvements with this format.

Recently when I was taking photos at Victoria Peak, I met six photographers, lined up and shooting the same location. All of them were using 4x5 or panorama cameras. They told me they were reshooting because their clients refused to pay for the digital shots they had taken, even though the digital cameras they had used were reliable brands such as Nikon and Canon.

Some of the photos in this book are shot with a 35mm camera, although all the large, double-page spreads were captured using a panorama camera. The difference in quality is significant, especially in unfavourable weather conditions.

Fumio Okada

Wong Tai Sin Temple

Ornate urn and sculpture stand in front of a busy temple decorated with red lanterns.
Named after Taoist deity Wong Tai Sin, the temple is one of the most notable in Hong Kong.

Nathan Road

Colourful shop signs abound on this busy Kowloon road, their reflections distorted in a bus window.

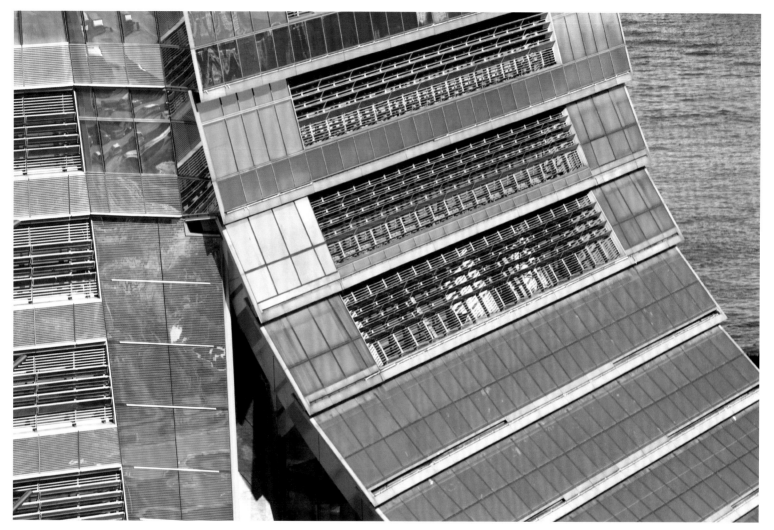

ICC Building

Taken from a rarely seen angle, a panel running down the side of the ICC appears to unfold like an accordion.

ICC Building and Kowloon Station Complex

The ICC stands proudly against an azure sky. Rising 484 metres it is Hong Kong's tallest building.

Little Oranges

Visitors shop for Kumquat Trees at the Tsuen Wan Flower Market. Traditionally sold just before
Chinese New Year, the tiny oranges have an edible sweet rind and citrus aroma.

Jade Market

Beautiful jade necklaces hang ready to be admired at a stall in the Jade Market, Yau Ma Tei.

Beads of Beauty

Tourists at the Jade Market peruse a colourful stall dominated by vibrant red. Selling jade of all descriptions, the market is one of Kowloon's most renowned.

Harbour at Dusk

As the sun begins to set, buildings along the Tsim Sha Tsui waterfront glisten like golden statues and spectacular clouds of purple, pink and white take shape.

Hong Kong THE DIVERSITY OF CULTURES 2

Restricted View

The view of a Shenzhen condominium taken from Sha Tau Kok. A restricted area until February 2012, Sha Tau Kok is one of only six formerly restricted areas now open to visitors, who can only gain access with a special visa.

Childs Play

Children on bicycles race down a hillside and past an old village house in Sha Tau Kok. The village
has topography that is not seen in town areas.

Tucked Away in Time

In a rural village in Sha Tau Kok, old houses sit sleepily amongst trees, oblivious to the modernisation going on around them.

Village Elder

An old Hakka woman stops to rest outside a village home in Sha Tau Kok. Her mild and gentle features typify Hakka people from this village, who have a history here that dates back a few hundred years.

Hippies and Worshipers

While locals line up to pay their respects, a young hippie couple get into the spirit of the Bun Festival outside a temple on Cheung Chau Island.

Tintin in China

Shown at an exhibition, a colourful illustration shows Tintin and his faithful dog Snowy on a rickshaw
ride through an old fashioned Chinese street.

Pedder Street at Night

By night Central is void of its myriad corporate workers, tourists and shoppers, leaving bright lights and a blur of traffic to set a new pace.

Hong Kong THE DIVERSITY OF CULTURES 2

Low-rise High-rise

Old low-rise homes sit in quiet contrast to a new high-rise block in Quarry Bay.

Big Brothers

Illuminated by bright lights, the ICC in Kowloon stands out against a beautiful dark night sky. Across the harbour, its little brother the IFC strikes an equally impressive pose, with lights shimmering for all to admire.

Ma Wan Fishing Village

Fishing boats and fish farms float on a peaceful sea, presenting a tranquillity that contradicts the busy redevelopment of this area.

Last Moments

Once teeming with life, this old village in Ma Wan, northeast Lantau, is now deserted. Dating back 250 years it will soon be demolished.

Repulse Bay

In good weather locals and visitors flock to the clean, sandy beaches of this crescent-shaped bay
on the south side of Hong Kong. Luxury apartments, including the uniquely shaped Lily designed by
Norman Foster, look down on sunbathers.

I Love T-shirts

Abundant in all manner of clothing and accessories, the Ladies Market in Mongkok is a shopping haven for tourists.

What Shop Signs?

In Mongkok, shoppers wander through streets oblivious to the myriad shop signs hanging just above their heads.

Victoria Harbour Skyline at Dusk

Viewed from Kowloon, buildings along the Hong Kong side of the harbour glisten in the disappearing sunlight. Behind them the undulating hills of the Peak and, in the foreground, calm harbour waters host only a few visitors.

Hong Kong THE DIVERSITY OF CULTURES 2

Chuk Lam Shim Yuen Monastery

The beautiful rooftop of the Bamboo Forest Monastery, so named because it is surrounded by a
bamboo grove. Located in Tsuen Wan, in the New Territories, it was founded in 1927.

Little Dragon Heads

The Chuk Lam Shim Yuen Monastery has many traditional Chinese features, such as this one with small dragon heads.

Lion Dance

A colourful lion prepares to dance at the Tai Mui Tin Hau Temple, also known as Joss House Bay Temple. In Chinese culture the Lion Dance has a history of almost a thousand years.

Dragon Boat Race,
Aberdeen and Po Tai Island

Teams race to the finish line. Sat two-abreast in boats with
dragon head and tail, paddlers are urged on by the beat
set by the drummer at the prow.

Day Off

On their day of rest Filipinas gather in Central to dance with friends.

Community Steps

The steps on Shelley Street in Soho are a popular place for expatriate families to gather and chit-chat. The steps run parallel to the Mid-levels escalator, the longest outdoor covered escalator in the world.

Opposite Directions

Taken from Ma Wan Island, this photograph shows westward bound Tsing Ma Bridge on the right. Part of the Lantau Link that connects Hong Kong with the International Airport, it is the longest road and rail suspension bridge in the world. On the left, the Ting Kau Bridge leads northwest to the New Territories and mainland China.

Hong Kong THE DIVERSITY OF CULTURES 2

Container Terminal, Kwai Chung

Cargo waits to be forwarded to various destinations from one of the largest and busiest ports in the world.

Two Bridges, One Impossible View

From this unusual angle, the Tsing Ma and Ting Kau Bridges appear to run parallel to each other and look as though they are one. A huge gulf of water separates the two bridges, which carry passengers in opposite directions. This rare view is captured from a location most do not know and is the only position from where the bridges can be seen like this.

Fishing Boat

Armed with a red net held by spider-like legs, a fishing vessel heads out in search of a fresh catch in the waters around Cheung Chau Island.

Wholesale Fruit Market

Surrounded by modern apartment blocks, old corrugated rooftops house part of the market in Yau Ma Tei. Built in 1913, around 240 stalls continue to trade fresh fruit daily.

Boats Moored

Small fishing boats and junks moor alongside each other at an old village in Sai Kung. Once a fishing village, Sai Kung attracts many with its seafood restaurants.

Stonecutters Bridge

Ten years in the making Stonecutters Bridge opened in 2009. Spanning 1,018 metres it is the second longest cable-stayed bridge in the world. From this unique angle the stay-cables fan out from their concrete and steel support tower like a sculptural work of art.

View from the Peak

The harbour bathes in the magical light of dusk. Looming in the foreground, the International Finance Centre (IFC) in Central faces the ICC on the opposite side of the harbour.

Hong Kong THE DIVERSITY OF CULTURES 2

Causeway Bay

Billboards and shops signs hang above trams, buses and cars as they weave their way through one of the most densely packed areas in Hong Kong.

Billboards

Causeway Bay is a shopping mecca. If the fashion-conscious are unsure of what to buy, they only need glance at the enormous billboards and advert-clad buses for a clue.

Cross Roads

Traffic stands still as a blur of pedestrians cross roads in busy Causeway Bay.

Kung Ting Study Hall

The surrounding walls of the study hall in Ping Shan, Yuen Long. Built in the 1870s the hall sits amongst comparatively modern low-rise housing.

Nam Pin Wai Village

When strolling down a village lane in Yuen Long, it is typical to see washing hanging above doorways, bicycles at the ready and plastic chairs waiting to be sat upon. These are part of village life.

New Position

The new Central Government Offices in Admiralty has a shiny glass façade. Outside freshly planted
trees and lawn take hold.

Chung King Mansion

Built in 1961, Chung King is renowned for its cheap guest houses, Indian restaurants, and mix of
backpackers and ethnic residents. It has always had a seedy reputation, and was immortalised
as a den of lawlessness in the Wong Kar Wai movie Chungking Express. Recently, its façade was
refurbished and is now clean and shiny. The inside however remains just the same!

1881 Heritage, Tsim Sha Tsui

Illuminated at night, the face of this former Marine Police Headquarters still presents characteristics of
its colonial past. Built in the 1880s, it underwent a 6-year revitalisation process to re-emerge in 2009
complete with luxury shops, fine dining and hotel.

Hong Kong THE DIVERSITY OF CULTURES 2

Quiet Moment

A quiet village lane in Nam Pin Wai village, Yuen Long, provides the perfect spot for this village elder to sit and ponder life.

Nam Pin Wai Village

The traditional architecture of an entrance to a walled village in Yuen Long stands out against modern homes. Built in 1669, Nam Pin Wai is one of the few remaining walled villages in Hong Kong.

St. John's Cathedral, Central

Planted with beautiful trees and gardens, the cathedral offers a peaceful respite from the high-rise
metropolis that surrounds it. Dating back to 1849 it is the oldest Anglican church in the Far East and
a declared Hong Kong monument.

Giant Buddha

Perched atop the Ngong Ping plateau on Lantau Island, visitors must climb more than 200 steps to reach the majestic seated Buddha.

Hong Kong **THE DIVERSITY OF CULTURES 2**

Bun Festival, Cheung Chau

Constructed beneath scaffolding and colourful banners, large bamboo towers are studded with sweet white buns. Crowds gather in anticipation of watching participants race up the towers in a contest to grab the luckiest buns from the very top. Practised for more than 100 years, this annual festival is a spectacle of immense fun!

Dragon Dance

Captured in motion, a colourful Dragon dances at the Tam Kung
Festival in Shau Kei Wan.
The event marks the birthday of Tam Kung, saint of seafarers said
to bring security and happiness to all fishermen.

Dragon Handlers

Long and sinuous, each Dragon has a team of handlers. Here the
creatures are being herded at the Tam Kung Festival.

Panoramic Harbour View

Taken from the back of a ferry, this spectacular panoramic photograph captures both sides of the
harbour beneath a beautiful, clear indigo sky.

HongKong THE DIVERSITY OF CULTURES 2

The Lion Rocks

Perched in on a hill in the Lion Rock Country Park, the Lion Rock is granite. Songs and books have been written about the 'Crouching Lion'. It also served as inspiration for a long-running TV series.

Hong Kong THE DIVERSITY OF CULTURES 2

Hong Kong Geopark

An area of breathtaking beauty, the Geopark in Sai Kung is home to unique rock types found in only three other places in the world.

The Blue House

Located in Wanchai, the iconic Blue House will soon undergo renovations to become a trendy art spot, and will remain painted blue.

Seldom Seen Side of the ICC

A cross screen filter was used when taking this unusual photograph of the ICC at night. The graphic, criss-cross lines made by tiny decorative rooftop lights juxtapose the buildings straight lines of brightly lit windows, creating a rare effect.

Nathan Road

Young shrubbery in front of old buildings clad with shop signs and scaffolding on one of Kowloon's busiest roads.

Anchored Fishing Boats

Often lived on by fishermen, these fishing boats snuggle together safely anchored at Shaukiwan
Typhoon Shelter.

Colonial Nathan Road

Dubbed 'Nathan's Folly' after Sir Matthew Nathan, Governor of Hong Kong, 1904-1907, this photograph shows a quiet Nathan Road lined with colonial buildings.

Neon on Nathan Road

Traffic becomes an artistic blur under the neon signs of one of the busiest roads in Kowloon.

Star Cruise, Star Ferry

A frequent visitor to Hong Kong harbour, the enormous Star Cruise ship towers above a passing Star Ferry.

Ad-clad Tram

Hong Kong trams, such as this one parked in Shaukiwan Tram Terminal, are used as moving billboards to advertise myriad products.

Ngong Ping 360 Cable Car

Sightseers enjoy clear views on a sunny day. The 25-minute cable car ride offers spectacular views of
the Lantau countryside and Hong Kong International Airport.

Buddha and Bubbles

The Tian Tan Buddha (Big Buddha) sits serenely as blown bubbles gently float in front of the camera lens, creating a magical effect.

Sheung Shui

Situated in the New Territories on the border with China, this photograph shows one of the last remaining old areas left amidst the renovated and the rebuilt.

Mongkok Billboard

Enormous billboards like these are highly fashionable in Hong Kong.

Lei Yu Mun Village

Gently snuggled beneath trees, stilt-houses line the waterfront of this quaint old village. Lei Yu Mun is a short channel that separates Hong Kong and Kowloon, and serves as the east gate to Victoria harbour.

Hong Kong THE DIVERSITY OF CULTURES 2

Pigs Don't Fly

A pig being delivered to the Yau Ma Tei food market. A common sight in Hong Kong, only the child
in this photograph seems remotely interested.

Traditional Entrance

An ornate Chinese-style gateway in Yau Ma Tei proudly announces Temple Street.

Street Dining, Yau Ma Tei Style

Local Hong Kongers enjoy alfresco dining at a sidewalk restaurant.

Street Dining, Stanley Style

Expatriates enjoy alfresco dining outside a restaurant of a different kind.

Hong Kong THE DIVERSITY OF CULTURES 2

Cat Street

Located just off of Hollywood Road in Central, Cat Street has myriad shops and outdoor stalls selling
trinkets, curios and collectables. A quaint street, it attracts locals and tourists alike.

Shop 469

KOOKAÏ

Shatin Shopping Plaza

The plaza attracts consumers with fashionable shops selling equally fashionable clothing.

The Pen Circa 2012

Built in 1928, The Peninsula Hotel is the city's oldest hotel. Fondly dubbed the 'Grande Dame', the stately 5-star hotel sits alongside shiny new buildings and pedestrian-heavy Nathan Road. In 1994 a 30-storey tower topped with a helipad was added. Over the next year further renovations and upgrades are planned.

The Pen Circa 1930

An aerial view of the hotel in 1930, two years after it opened. Its ritzy marble lobby became a favourite rendezvous for wealthy tycoons. Under Japanese occupation it was renamed Tōa Hotel by Japanese soldiers who used it as their headquarters.

Traditional Design in Orange

An ornate orange temple roof at the Yuen Yuen Institute in Lo Wai stands out against lush green foliage.

Lee Gardens

Above the Lee Gardens a skyscraper filled with offices bursts into the night sky. The Lee Gardens houses upscale, high-end shopping boutiques favoured by lovers of big-brand names.

Ladder Street

Connecting Queens Road with Hollywood Road, this aptly named row of steep steps in Sheung Wan provides a light workout.

Nina Tower

All gleaming glass and metal structures, this photograph captures Nina's curvaceous side. Nina Tower is actually two towers that sit on a 9-storey podium. Totalling 90 storeys it resides on the waterfront at Tsuen Wan.

Wing Lee Street, Central

Washing hangs in front of 'tong lau' (walk-up) buildings dating back to the 1950s. Due to be demolished, interest in these houses increased after they featured in the film Echoes of the Rainbow directed by Alex Law, which won a Berlin Film Festival award in 2010. Now all 12 houses will be preserved.

Harbour Panorama

Buildings on the Hong Kong side of the harbour cast pretty colours on velvet-like waters and twinkle like jewels in this magnificent panoramic image taken at night.

Chinese Clinic

Old buildings such as this are now few and far between in Wanchai.

Replica

In the 1980s the Sung Dynasty Village theme park entertained visitors with acrobats, dancers and actors dressed in traditional period costumes. Handicraft stalls, a wax museum and replica bars such as the one pictured here recreated the era. The village has since been demolished.

Cross Street Market

Stalls are shaded by colourful parasols. The Wanchai market sells all manner of goods, from clothes and jade jewellery to dried and fresh fruits.

Nightlife in Wanchai

Lined with a plethora of bars, Lockhart Road draws many expats in search of cheap beer and loud chit-chat.

Incense Shop

Colourful and fragrant shops selling incense are common place in many areas. This one in West
Point also sells items such as cars made from paper for burning at funerals. This ensures those
passing have all the mod-cons they need in the afterlife.

Dried Goods

The Western District has a multitude of shops selling all sorts of dried items, from sea urchins, fish and shark fins to fungi, herbs and tea. These pungent shops attract tourists and buyers from mainland China.

Skyscrapers Galore

In this view from the Peak, skyscrapers rise into the sky as if in competition. The IFC takes first prize on Hong Kong Island, while across the harbour ICC dominates.

Master Pui To Grotto

Protected in a cave at the Tsing Shan Monastery in the New Territories, this small shrine is dedicated to Master Pui To, a Buddhist monk who travelled carrying a big wooden cup. His name translates as 'Travelling in a Cup'.

Golden Buddha Statues

Preserved behind glass at the Chuk Lam Shim Yuen Monastery, beautiful golden Buddha statues are offered flowers and fruit as a mark of respect.

Incense

Incense burning outside the Pak Tei Temple on Cheung Chau Island. Producing a fragrant smoke,
incense is burned to dispel negativity and create a calm, pure atmosphere. As it rises and dissolves
into the air, it also serves as a reminder of the transient nature of existence.

Dragon Heads

Dragon heads greet visitors at the Tsing Chung Koon Temple in Tuen Mun. They can also be seen atop a temple rooftop at this Taoist temple built in 1961.

Temple Guards

Visitors approaching the Po Lin Monastery on Lantau Island are watched over by statues of fierce-looking guards.

Reclining Buddha

A beautiful reclining Buddha lays on a bed of hand painted lotus leaves at the Western Monastery,
just a short walk from the Yuen Yuen Institute at Lo Wai Village in Tsuen Wan.

Hong Kong THE DIVERSITY OF CULTURES 2

Victoria Harbour 1970

Busy harbour traffic is captured in a tapestry of colourful threads. Illuminated buildings along the waterfront cast neon shades across the water and, in the background, tiny lights outline the Peak.

Victoria Harbour 2012

Obscuring most of the Peak, skyscrapers ablaze with bright lights dominate the skyline. Minimal harbour traffic creates a few painterly red strands across its silky surface.

Quiet Spot to Fish

The undulating hills, lush mangrove bushes and calm waters at Luk Keng in the New Territories next to China typify this bucolic area.

Setting Sail

Yachts with brightly coloured sails race around Victoria Harbour passing Lei Yu Mun, the east gate of the harbour.

Fantasy City

This stunning photograph was created through a process created using an advanced technique used only by Daiichi some 30 years ago – before the birth of Apple Macs! The technique combines real photography with time-consuming retouching.

Fantasy Plane

Created using the same method as the previous image. The background image is a real photograph and the aeroplane a model. Each tiny detail on the plane and runway were created by computer, taking countless hours. The plane is super imposed onto the photo to create this superbly clear yet surreal image of a plane landing at Kai Tak Airport.

Ding Ding!

Colourful trams trundle along Des Voeux Road in Central. They are affectionately called Ding Dings because of the sound of their bell, which is triggered by the foot of the driver.

Colonial Trams

With its plush hotels and upscale shops, Des Voeux Road was a mecca for shoppers. Double-decker trams presented a convenient way to hop from shop to shop, but added to road congestion.

Chinese Opera

Staged outdoors on a bamboo set, this Chiu Chow-style folk opera celebrates the annual Hungry Ghost Festival. It is held in July when the spirits of ancestors return and are offered food by the living.

Nightlife in Civic Square

Located above Kowloon Station an open area boasting bars, restaurants and bright lights attracts
visitors to sit and chit-chat while they wine and dine.

ICC from Civic Square

Visitors that come to enjoy the dining facilities at Civic Square also enjoy the view of the ICC lit up
at night.

Streets of Gold

Aerial shot taken from the ICC's viewing platform, the Sky100. Prior to this viewing platform, panoramic aerial photos could only be taken by helicopter. To do this at night with a hand-held camera was virtually impossible. Here, roads in Kowloon appear to be made of liquid gold.

Panorama Drama

Also taken from the Sky100 viewing platform at the ICC, this 180-degree view looks over the
Kowloon peninsula. In this sprawling urban landscape buildings are tinged by the cool blue light of
dusk.

Hong Kong THE DIVERSITY OF CULTURES 2

Fireworks

Taken from the ICC in Kowloon, an explosion of fireworks lights up the Hong Kong harbourside.

Friends in High Places

This view showing the beautiful architecture of the ICC is not seen by many as it is taken from a private garden in one of the surrounding apartment blocks.

Crystal Clear

A stunning180-degree view of Hong Kong Island spanning the IFC in Central to Quarry Bay in the north. Taken from the top of the ICC in Kowloon. Captured just before sunset, buildings along the Tsim Sha Tsui waterfront shimmer with clarity.

Hong Kong THE DIVERSITY OF CULTURES 2

Cannons

Three of the remaining six cannons on the north wall of the Tung Chung Fort, which dates back to 1832. The cannons face out to sea and were used to protect the island against pirates.

Brick-Lined Tomb

Discovered in 1955, the Li Cheung Uk Han Tomb is believed to date back to the Eastern Han dynasty, AD 25-200. If walls could talk, what stories this ancient tomb could tell!

Soft Light

Couples come to the steps on Duddell Street in Central to have wedding photos taken beneath the soft light cast from the city's only two remaining gas lamps. Erected between 1975 and 1889, both steps and gas lamps are declared monuments.

No Flash Required

Presumed to cast only a soft light, gas lamps also produce bright light,
as seen in this photograph where no flash was used.

Hong Kong THE DIVERSITY OF CULTURES 2

Well Preserved

A classical Edwardian building, the façade of the Dr. Sun Yat-sen Museum features beautiful red bricks and Greek-style columns. Inside houses well-preserved stained-glass windows and period wall tiles.

Pawn Shop

A well-kept 1950s-style pawn shop in Shanghai Street, Yau Ma Tei. Not many of these still exist, but the few that remain are clearly recognisable by their unique sign, which is shaped like a bat, signifying fortune, holding a coin, a symbol of benefits.

Wondrous Flats

Located in the far northeast corner of Hong Kong, Tung Ping Chau is a crescent-shaped island renowned for its unique rock formations. It is the only island in Hong Kong made up of sedimentary rock, which creates these stunning flat rocks.

Mooring at Sai Kung

Sai Kung is a popular weekend destination. Many head out on junk boats, arriving in time to enjoy lunch at one of the many seafood restaurants. The rest of the day is spent relaxing on the boat before slowly cruising home in the evening.

Traffic Jam

In a street in Yau Ma Tei shop signs hang as still as the cars stuck in the traffic beneath them.

Night Market

People casually wander, perusing all sorts of goods on sale at street stalls in Temple Street.

Fresh Catch

A busy stall in the wet market at Tai Kok Tsui in Kowloon displays a daily catch of fresh fish and seafood.

Wine Festival

Wine bottles with artfully designed labels sit on display at a wine festival held at the West Kowloon
Waterfront Promenade.

Sketching by the Sea

An artist sketches boats along the seashore at Shaukeiwan typhoon shelter.

Equestrian Fun

Urged on by their jockeys, horses gallop at full speed to reach the finish line in a neck and neck race
at Happy Valley Racecourse.

Glorious Tangerine Sky

Viewed from the Peak the Western Harbour glows with tiny bright lights. Photographed at dusk, an impressive string of dark clouds roll across the Kowloon mountains while boats that look as if carved from onyx gather on deep blue waters.

Hong Kong THE DIVERSITY OF CULTURES 2

Index

p83　　p84　　p85　　p86　　p87　　p88　　p90　　p91　　p92

p93　　p94　　p95　　p96　　p97　　p98　　p99　　p99　　p100　　p101

p102　　p104　　p105　　p106　　p107　　p108　　p109　　p110

p112　　p113　　p114　　p115　　p116　　p117　　p118　　p118

p120　　p121　　p122　　p123　　p124　　p125　　p126　　p128　　p129

p130　　p132　　p134　　p135　　p136　　p138　　p139

p140　　p140　　p141　　p142　　p143　　p144　　p146　　p147　　p148　　p148

p149　　p150　　p151　　p152　　Back Endpaper

Hong Kong **THE DIVERSITY OF CULTURES 2**

Published by Daiichi Publishers Co. Ltd.

ISBN: 978-988-99143-9-4

All enquires to:
Daiichi Publishers Co. Ltd.
Unit 22, 8/F, Zung Fu Ind. Bldg.
1067 King's Road, Quarry Bay
Hong Kong
Tel: 2344 7007 Fax: 2343 4946
Email: info@daiichipublishers.com

Produced by Oriental Touch Ltd.
Editing by Virginia Ho

Written by Martine Beale
Designed by Eddie Cheung
Production & printing supervision by Fommy Fong

Colour separations by Daiichi System Graphics
Company Ltd.
Printed by Paramount Printing Co., Ltd.

Printed in Hong Kong